winter's grace

A CANTATA FOR CHRISTMAS

...artin

Orchestration by ʙrant Adams

CONTENTS

(1) This symbol indicates a track number on the StudioTrax CD (Accompaniment Only).

Harold Flammer MUSIC

A DIVISION OF SHAWNEE PRESS, INC.
EXCLUSIVELY DISTRIBUTED BY HAL LEONARD CORPORATION

Visit Shawnee Press Online at
www.shawneepress.com

FOREWORD

Each year, as winter takes hold and covers our days with its silent wonder, we are called to reflection. As the shadows grow longer and the nights deepen, we gather in our chapels of faith seeking the comfort found in the assurance of God's Word.

We light our candles of hope. We sing our songs of gathering. We read the ancient words of the prophets and cling to every promise like a quivering leaf on a fading branch.

Then Christmas comes sweeping into our fading hope with its jubilant glorias and peaceful carols of love. The darkened mangers of our hearts are transformed into cradles of light, and we surrender our doubts and fears for the shining joy of star-shine and angel-song. We awaken to mystery and miracles. We embrace the beautiful impossible of heaven on earth. We find the heart of Christ waiting for us like a sanctuary of life.

And so in the bleak mid-winter we gather to worship at the cradle of the newborn King. We cast away our sin and our sorrows. We put away all of life's burdens and distractions. With our arms and hearts emptied of all earthly clutter, we can now freely reach for our gift… and it reaches back to us. It is grace… and it is wrapped in a baby named Jesus.

JOSEPH M. MARTIN

PROGRAM NOTES

Winter's Grace tells the Christmas story using music, Scripture, prayers and poetry. Similar poetic motives are presented to tie the work together, using snow and other seasonal imagery to represent humankind's spiritual need for renewal and redemption.

The opening poem, "The Snow," may be read aloud from off stage, simply placed in the worship folder or projected on sanctuary screens as a contemplative preparation for this cantata's presentation.

The opening solo may be sung from memory as the soloist processes to the front of the sanctuary. Following this, the transitional poem, "Tis Winter Now the Falling Snow" is read as the soloist lights candles around the chancel area, creating atmosphere and drama as the cantata unfolds.

As each carol is presented, the sanctuary may be gradually adorned with the congregation's traditional holiday decorations. Elements such as the Advent candles should be synchronized carefully with an appropriate corresponding anthem, such as "Hope, Peace, Love and Joy." Other options may become apparent as you further consider this work.

A nativity scene may be placed on the altar and appropriate characters may be added (shepherds, angels, wise men, etc.) as the story line unfolds. Some congregations may want to include a live nativity gathering or even incorporate a scrim or other theatrical elements. What is important is to allow the scene to reveal itself gradually in tandem with the appropriate music.

If a tree is to be included, consider using "Chrismons" to decorate it gradually, as each musical piece is presented. See the "Digital Resource Kit" for ornament designs related to this tradition. Many members of the congregation, including children, can help to create these meaningful symbols in preparation for the cantata's presentation. They can also participate in hanging these ornaments as the story unfolds.

It is recommended that the final lighting of the tree be reserved for the final movement, "Silent Night." As this beloved carol is sung, the worship space will be visually transformed; representing God's transforming Gift of Grace, born into our world. The world's spiritual "winter" has been redeemed by the miraculous birth of Jesus, our Savior!

These are merely a few suggestions to enhance your sharing of *Winter's Grace*. You are welcome to adapt this work, at your own discretion, to your congregation's traditions. As always, these elements are all optional as I have made certain that this cantata will also stand alone, without any extra-musical additions.

JOSEPH M. MARTIN

THE SNOW

Folding the earth in its mantle
Pure and undefiled,
Soft in its own clear whiteness
As the cheek of an innocent child,
The snow o'er the world is falling,
It floats upon the air,
Silent, yet ever restless,
As a child's hands crossed in prayer.

Like a benediction descending
O'er the sin-stained weary world,
It falls in tender pity,
Its mantle o'er all unfurled.
Oh, Father in Heaven above us,
Thy goodness and Thy love
Descend like a silent spirit,
Like a pure and spotless dove.

This world is a myst'ry of sorrow,
And dark with sin and woe;
Over its toil and sadness
Thy mantle of mercy throw.
Fold us about, protect us
In Thy garment, spotless white,
As the snow in its silent falling
Is shrouding the earth tonight.

Edith Willis Linn Forbes (1865-1945)

WINTER'S GRACE
Prologue

Words by
CHRISTINA ROSSETTI (1830-1894)

Tune: **CRANHAM**
GUSTAV HOLST (1874-1934)
Arranged by
JOSEPH M. MARTIN (BMI)

* Tune: CRANHAM, Gustav Holst, 1874-1934
Words: Christina Rossetti, 1830-1894

WINTER'S GRACE - SAT(

snow____ on____ snow. In the bleak mid -

win - ter, long,____ long a - go,

long,____ long a - go!____

8

* 'Tis winter now. The fallen snow
has left the heavens all coldly clear.

Through leafless boughs the sharp winds blow,
and all the earth lies dead and drear.

And yet God's love is not withdrawn.
His life within the keen air breathes.

His beauty paints the crimson' dawn,
and clothes the boughs with glitt'ring wreaths.

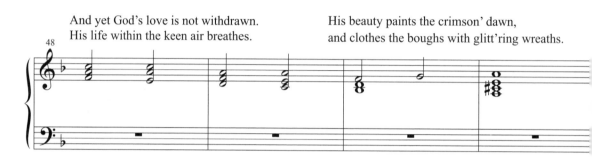

And though abroad, the sharp winds blow,
and skies are chill, and frosts are keen;

home closer draws her circle now,
and warmer glows her light within.

O God, who giv'st the winter's cold
as well as summer's joyous rays,

us warmly in Thy love enfold,
and keep us through life's wintry days!

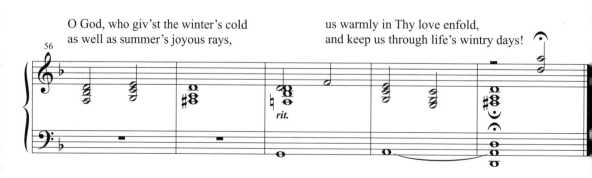

* "Hymn of Winter" by Samuel Longfellow, 1819-1892

WINTER'S GRACE - SATB

A WINTER'S SONG

Words and music by
JOSEPH M. MARTIN (BMI)

From ___ an - cient ___ times ___ the proph - ets ___ spoke a - gainst the win - ter's moan. When will God ___ send ___ forth ___ His ___ Morn - ing ___ Star to ___

* Tenors may double Alto *sotto voce* measures 45-50.

14

Lyrics (SATB):

fall. As win-ter sings her__ sol-emn song, we

Shad-ows soon will fall.

long to hear Love's call.___ A-

rise, a-wake, the__ time is here. Christ will come to__

Oo___

win - ter now. The fall - ing snow has__ left the heav - ens

clear. Through__ leaf - less boughs the

sharp winds blow. All the earth lies dead and

drear;   and___   yet   God's   love   is

not   with - drawn   for___   beau - ty   paints   the___

crim - son   dawn!_____   Come,   O

rit.   *a tempo*

a tempo

rit.

18

THE WORD OF THE LORD

Hear the promise of God:

The people who walk in darkness will see a great light. For those who live in a land of deep shadows, a light will shine! (Isaiah 9:2)

PRAYER

Let us pray:

Come to us Light of the World. From deep in our darkness, we lift our longing hearts to You.

Come, O Dayspring, come to our world and warm us with Your radiant grace.

O Sun of Righteousness, shine upon our path and show us the way everlasting.

Bright and Morningstar, bring to those who live in the winter of despair Your shining hope.

Come Immanuel and abide with us, and decorate our lives with Your joy and peace.

CELEBRATION FOR ADVENT

Words by
JOSEPH M. MARTIN (BMI)

Based on tunes
RIU, RIU, CHIU
VENI EMMANUEL
and **NOEL NOUVELET**
Arranged by
JOSEPH M. MARTIN (BMI)

Ve - ni, ve - ni, ve - ni. Come,___ Lord of the na - tions.___

* Tune: RIU, RIU, CHIU; Traditional Spanish Carol

Ve - ni, ve - ni, ve - ni. Bring___ us Thy sal - va - tion.___

Ve - ni, ve - ni, ve - ni, day___ of cel - e - bra - tion.___

Ve - ni, ve - ni. Come and set our hearts___ to ju - bi - la - tion.

Ve - ni, ve - ni, ve - ni. Come and set our hearts___ to ju - bi - la - tion.

22

* Tune: VENI EMMANUEL, 15th century plainsong
  Words: Latin Hymn; tr. John Mason Neale, 1818-1866

WINTER'S GRACE - SAT

54

Re - joice! Re -

f

pears.

Re - joice!

f

55

joice!

Re - joice! Em - man - u - el shall

58

10

come to Thee, O Is - ra - el!

Peo - ple of the prom - ise, peace be___ yours to -

night._____ All who wait in dark - ness

* Tune: NOEL NOUVELET, Traditional French Carol

WINTER'S GRACE - SATB

26

Ve - ni, ve - ni, ve - ni. Come,___ Lord of the na - tions.___

_ Ve - ni, ve - ni, ve - ni. Bring___ us Thy sal - va - tion.

with great drive and power

f *unis.*

with great drive and power

THE WORD OF THE LORD

Hear the Word of the Lord:

The Dayspring from on high has visited us, to give light to those who sit in darkness and the shadow of death, to guide our feet into the way of peace. (Luke 1: 78b-79)

PRAYER

Let us pray:

God of glory and eternal light, as we light these candles for hope, peace, love and joy, we remember that You alone are the source of all things bright and good. You alone illuminate the world with golden promise, and it is Your fire alone that burns in our hearts with the spirit of truth and grace. Help us to be Your candles and let us give ourselves in service to Your eternal flame.

commissioned by the Church Family of Bethesda United Methodist Church, Salisbury, MD
in honor and appreciation of Dr. Douglas J. Smith's
untiring and dedicated 25 years of service as Director of Music

HOPE, PEACE, JOY AND LOVE

Words and music by
JOSEPH M. MARTIN (BMI)

* Available separately: 35009665

burn - ing in the night.

p unis.

Hope paints ev - 'ry

shad - ow with its gen - tle light.

Glow - ing like a prom - ise till our faith is

WINTER'S GRACE - SATB

sight.   Hope   is   like   a____   can - dle   in   the

night.   Peace   is   like   sweet

mu - sic   sound - ing   pure   and   strong,_____

36

WINTER'S GRACE - SATB

Lyrics:
mu - sic pure and strong.

Joy is like a flow - er bloom - ing in the soul,

send - ing forth its fra - grance to

And when bit - ter winds are

heal and make us whole.

blow - ing, when birds re - fuse to sing,

joy can turn our win - ter in - to spring.

sold. Pearl of heav - en's glo - ry,

bought or sold.

won - drous to be - hold,

love is like a___

dia - mond wrapped in gold.___

40

THE WORD OF THE LORD

Hear the Word of the Lord:

And I will give you a sign: a virgin will conceive and give birth to a Son. And will call His name Immanuel. (Isaiah 7:10-14)

Now hear the promise fulfilled:

In the sixth month the angel Gabriel was sent from God to a city of Galilee named Nazareth, to a virgin betrothed to a man whose name was Joseph, of the house of David. And the virgin's name was Mary.

And he came to her and said, "Greetings, O favored one, the Lord is with you!"

But she was greatly troubled at the saying, and tried to discern what sort of greeting this might be.

And the angel said to her, "Do not be afraid, Mary, for you have found favor with God. And behold, you will conceive in your womb and bear a Son, and you shall call His name Jesus. He will be great and will be called the Son of the Most High. And the Lord God will give to Him the throne of His father David, and He will reign over the house of Jacob forever, and of His kingdom there will be no end." (Luke 1:26-33)

PRAYER

Let us pray:

O Giver of Life, place in us Your holy presence. Create in us a beautiful sanctuary for Your Spirit of Truth. Let our hearts beat as one as we learn to trust Your purpose for our lives. As Your grace grows stronger in us every day, let us live to serve, and with humble hearts, deliver to the world Your gospel of peace.

CAROLS OF ADORATION

Based on tune,
VENITE ADOREMUS
and **GESU BAMBINO**
Arranged by
JOSEPH M. MARTIN (BMI

* Tune: VENITE ADOREMUS, Traditional English Carol
Words: Traditional English Carol

44

ni - te a - do - re - mus Do - mi - num.

(play)

18 molto rit. mp 32 A little slower, but still flowing (♩. = ca. 60)

*When blos - soms flow - ered 'mid_ the snows up -

32 A little slower, but still flowing (♩. = ca. 60)

molto rit. mp

on a win - ter night_ mf

was

* Tune: GESU BAMBINO, Pietro Yon, 1886-1943
Words: Frederick H. Martens, 1874-1932

WINTER'S GRACE - SATB

Lyrics:

born ____ the Child, __ the Christ - mas Rose, the King ___ of Love __ and Light.

The an - gels sang, __ the shep - herds sang, the re - joiced. ____

grate - ful earth __ re - joiced, re-joiced, cre - a - tion re - joiced. And

46

at___ His bless - ed birth the stars___ their ex - ul - ta - tion

voiced: ___

voiced, the stars re - joiced: ___ "O

come, let us a - dore___ Him. O

47

come, let us a - dore Him. O

come, let us a - dore Him, _____

Christ _____ the Lord."

WINTER'S GRACE - SATB

Light. Let ev - 'ry voice___ ac - claim His name, the

grate - ful cho - rus swell, the grate - ful cho - rus swell. From

par - a - dise___ to earth He came___ that we___ with Him might

113
S.
A.
T.
B.
Ah
p solo
pp
Oo
pp
Oo
pp
O
ni - te a - do - re - mus.
p
117
119
Oo
Oo
come, let us a - dore Him!
Ve - ni - te a - do - re - mus.

THE WORD OF THE LORD

Hear the Word of the Lord:

And it came to pass in those days, that there went out a decree from Caesar Augustus that all the world should be taxed. And all went to be taxed, every one into his own city. And Joseph also went up from Galilee, out of the city of Nazareth, into Judea, unto the city of David, which is called Bethlehem; (because he was of the house and lineage of David) to be taxed with Mary, his espoused wife, being great with Child.

And so it was, that, while they were there, the days were accomplished that she should be delivered. And she brought forth her firstborn Son, and wrapped Him in swaddling clothes, and laid Him in a manger; because there was no room for them in the inn.

And there were in the same country shepherds abiding in the field, keeping watch over their flock by night. And, lo, the angel of the Lord came upon them, and the glory of the Lord shone round about them: and they were sore afraid. And the angel said unto them: "Fear not: for, behold, I bring you good tidings of great joy, which shall be to all people. For unto you is born this day in the city of David a Savior, which is Christ the Lord. And this shall be a sign unto you; Ye shall find the babe wrapped in swaddling clothes, lying in a manger."

And suddenly there was with the angel a multitude of the heavenly host praising God, and saying: "Glory to God in the highest, and on earth peace, good will toward all." (Luke 2:1,3-14)

PRAYER

Let us pray:

Help us, O Lord, on this most wondrous of nights to listen with our hearts for the sounds of your coming. Let Your still small voice silence the clamor and noise of our selfishness and sin. Let us begin our journey to the manger with joyous abandon surrounded by the music of Your grace.

CAROLS OF PROMISE AND PRAISE

Original words by
JOSEPH M. MARTIN (BMI)

Based on tunes:
EL DESEMBRE CONGELAT
CHRISTMAS
GLORIA
and **HUMILITY**
Arranged by
JOSEPH M. MARTIN (BMI)

ACCOMP.

With graceful confidence (♩ = ca. 112)

* As the snow lay on the ground, frost-y winds were

* Tune: EL DESEMBRE CONGELAT, Traditional Catalan Carol
Words: Joseph M. Martin

56

blow - ing. Sud - den - ly there came_ a_ sound
from the heav - ens_ grow - ing. "Glo - ry_ be to_
God_ on_ high!"_
"Peace to all," they sang that night!_

WINTER'S GRACE - SATB

gin and___ nev - er cease,___ be - gin and___ nev - er

cease.

*An - gels we have___ heard on high, sweet - ly___ sing - ing

* Tune: GLORIA, Traditional French Carol
Words: Traditional French Carol

WINTER'S GRACE - SATB

-ri - a_____ in ex - cel - sis De - - o!

Glo - - - -

-ri - a in ex - cel - sis De -

62

* Tune: HUMILITY, John Goss, 1800-1880
Words: Edward Caswall, 1814-1878

WINTER'S GRACE - SATB

earth be - low; see, the ten - der Lamb ap-pears,

prom - ised from e - ter - nal years. Hail, thou ev - er

bless - ed morn! Hail, re-demp-tion's hap - py dawn!

Sing through all Je - ru - sa - lem:___ "Christ is born in

Beth - le - hem! Christ is born in Beth - le -

hem!"_____

THE WORD OF THE LORD

Hear the Word of the Lord:

When the angels went away from them into heaven, the shepherds said to one another, "Let us go over to Bethlehem and see this thing that has happened, which the Lord has made known to us." And they went with haste and found Mary and Joseph, and the baby lying in a manger. And when they saw it, they made known the saying that had been told them concerning this child. And all who heard it wondered at what the shepherds told them. But Mary treasured up all these things, pondering them in her heart. And the shepherds returned, glorifying and praising God for all they had heard and seen, as it had been told them.
(Luke 2:15-20)

PRAYER

Let us pray:

Exalted God, we acknowledge You as King of the universe and Lord of our lives. You have spoken Your word with all integrity and Your promise of grace will not be revoked. Through Your Son You have declared the great "AMEN" and at the sound of His name one day every knee will bow and every tongue confess that Jesus Christ is Lord.

LET THE EARTH RESOUND WITH PRAISE!

Words by
J. PAUL WILLIAMS (ASCAP)

Music by
JOSEPH M. MARTIN (BMI)
Incorporating tune:
SOMERSET CAROL

Christ is the King of kings, An-cient of Days!

Al-le-lu-ia! Al-le-lu-ia! Let the world re-sound with

Al - le - lu - ia!

praise!

70

Grace!_____ Al - le - lu - ia! Al - le - lu - ia! Let the world re-

Al - le - lu - ia!

sound with praise!

Come

Raise

all ye faith - ful, sing for joy and wor - ship Him in song.

* Tune: SOMERSET CAROL, Traditional English Carol

WINTER'S GRACE - SATB

honor, of glory__ and of praise. He is

wor - thy of hon - or, of glo - ry__ and of

praise.__

(end of descant)

Al - le - lu - ia! An-cient of Days!

Christ is the King of kings, An-cient of Days!

unis.

unis.

Al - le - lu - ia! Al - le - lu - ia! Let the world re -

sound   with   praise!_____

unis.

Let   the   world___ re - sound   with_____

praise!_____

THE WORD OF THE LORD

Hear the Word of the Lord:

After Jesus was born in Bethlehem in Judea, during the time of King Herod, Magi from the east came to Jerusalem and asked, "Where is the One who has been born King of the Jews? We saw His star in the east and have come to worship Him." (Matthew 2:1-2)

PRAYER

Let us pray:

O Guiding Light, like the magi of old we wander through the wilderness searching for answers to the great mysteries of the soul. We are Your seekers of the light, and we long to present to You the treasures of our heart. With humble thanks we bow and worship You.

*dedicated to the Centenary United Methodist Chancel Choir, McComb, Mississippi,
celebrating 125 years of faithful service, Epiphany 2009,
Rev. Patrick Schott, Director, and Bob Raborn, Pianist*

WHAT STRANGERS ARE THESE?

for S.A.T.B. voices, accompanied

Words:
Traditional Scottish Carol
adapted by
JOSEPH M. MARTIN

Traditional Scottish Tune
Arranged by
JOSEPH M. MARTIN (BMI)

78

cho - sen of the Lord, who will bear to all the prom - ised King. And who is this King of whom the an - gels sing? Know ye not the Christ, Je - sus the

Je - sus the Christ, Son__ of won - der. And what
fair maid is this filled with won - der and with awe? Oh, 'tis
Ma - ry, mild Moth-er of Je - sus. Oh,__

82

these are the shep-herds and these the Ma - gi Kings, who have brought Him their gifts of gold and myrrh._____ But____ why do they kneel_____ be - fore a ti - ny babe? They a -

dore their King, Je - sus the Sav - ior.

rit.

f *unis.*

Who are

f *unis.*

mf

rit.

44 With power and confidence (♩ = ca. 69)

these that____ march from death____ un - to life? These are

44 With power and confidence (♩ = ca. 69)

f

all who love Je - sus the Sav - ior. And____

how do they tri - umph o'er the gates of Hell? Through the

grace of Him, Je - sus the Sav - ior_____ He is

born to re-deem, let ev - 'ry heart re - joice! He brings

peace joy and love to all the world. Oh,___

where shall I find Him? Where___ shall I seek? He is

THE WORD OF THE LORD

Hear the Word of the Lord:

For to us a Child is born, to us a Son is given, and the government will be on His shoulders. And He will be called Wonderful Counselor, Mighty God, Everlasting Father, Prince of Peace. (Isaiah 9:6)

Now hear the words of Jesus, the Prince of Peace:

"I am leaving you with a gift – peace of mind and heart. And the peace I give is a gift the world cannot give. Let not your hearts be troubled, neither let them be afraid. (John 14:27)

in memory of the victims of the Kirkwood, Missouri, City Hall Shootings, February 7, 2008
and dedicated to community healing and reconciliation;
commissioned by the Music Ministry of Kirkwood United Methodist Church,
David Bennett, Senior Pastor; Dolan Bayless, Director of Music;
and Ronald and Patricia Krieger, Chancel Choir members

CANTICLE OF PEACE

Words and music by
JOSEPH M. MARTIN (BMI)

Peace, fall like a gen-tle snow.

Fall fresh on the wound-ed heart. Come blan-ket our

ev - 'ry fear and__ let the heal - ing start.

unis.

Cov - er ev - 'ry anx - ious thought, and all our fears e -

rase. May we know the__ ten - der touch of__

love's re - deem - ing grace.__

92

94

Do - na no - bis___ pa - cem,___

pa - cem.___

38

WINTER'S GRACE - SATB

THE FINAL BLESSING

And now grace and peace be yours in abundance through Christ our Lord. Through the gift of Jesus we have been provided everything we need for life. As the winter snow covers the barren earth with beauty, so His perfect grace has covered our sin with heaven's mercy. Hope, peace, joy and love are ours to claim and to share with others. His light and truth now shine within us guiding us through the journey of life.

And so now as we leave this sacred place may we hold these treasures near our hearts, always remembering: It is by grace that we are saved, through faith – and this not from ourselves, for grace is the perfect gift of God.

A SILENT, HOLY NIGHT

Words by
JOSEPH MOHR (1792-1848)

Tune: **STILLE NACHT**
by FRANZ GRUBER (1787-1863)
Arranged by
JOSEPH M. MARTIN (BMI)

* The first two measures may be played by a B♭ Handbell and may be repeated as desired.

Heav'n - ly hosts___ sing "Al - le - lu - ia,___

Christ the Sav - ior is born.___ Christ___ the Sav - ior is

born." Si - lent night,

(Accompanist may double voices if desired.)

ho - ly night, Son___ of God,___ love's pure light___

ra - diant beams___ from Thy ho - ly face,___ with___ the dawn of re -

deem - ing grace,___ Je - sus, Lord, at Thy birth,___

Je - sus, Lord, at Thy_ birth.